THINGS YOU SHOULD 10 KNOW ABOUT

BIG CATS

By Steve Parker
Illustrated by Ian Jackson

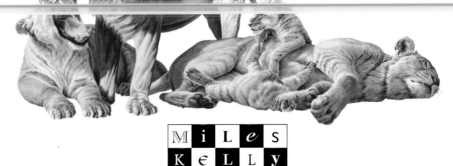

MILES KELLY
PUBLISHING

First published in 2002 by
Miles Kelly Publishing Ltd
Bardfield Centre,
Great Bardfield,
Essex, CM7 4SL

2 4 6 8 10 9 7 5 3 1

Editorial Director: Paula Borton
Art Director: Clare Sleven
Project Editor: Belinda Gallagher
Assistant Editors: Nicola Jessop, Nicola Sail
Designer: HERRING BONE DESIGN
Artwork Commissioning: Lesley Cartlidge
Indexer: Jane Parker

British Library Cataloguing-in-Publication Data
A catalogue record for this book is available
from the British Library

ISBN 1-84236-119-8

Printed in Hong Kong

www.mileskelly.net
info@mileskelly.net

Contents

Tigers are biggest

Cat facts
- The Siberian tiger measures 3.5 metres long, from nose to tail-tip.
- It weighs up to 300 kilograms – as much as five adult people.

The **SIBERIAN TIGER** is not just a big cat – it's the biggest cat! This huge hunter prowls the cold, snowy lands of Eastern Asia. It is the rarest kind of tiger, too, with less than 200 left in the wild. The Bengal tiger of the Indian region is more common, with about 5000 living wild.

The tiger has long fur on its cheeks, making its face look wide.

The Siberian tiger has thick fur to keep it warm in the ice and snow of winter.

Tigers have black stripes on their yellow, orange or gold fur. The Siberian tiger has more white in its coat to help it blend in with its snowy landscape.

Man-eaters!

Very rarely, tigers attack and eat people. These tigers are usually old or injured. They can't catch their normal prey such as deer, wild cattle and wild pigs.

The Siberian tiger is heavily built. Its body hangs close to the ground.

2 Pumas make good mothers

Cat facts
• The puma has a nose-to-tail length of 2.2 metres.
• It lives in western North America and South America.

Like all big cats, the female **PUMA** is a very caring mother. She protects her babies, feeds them on her milk — and keeps them warm and safe in a den.

Baby big cats are called cubs. Puma cubs have spotty coats when they are first born. These fade as they get older.

Puma cubs feed on their mother's milk for about seven weeks. Then they begin to eat pieces of meat which their mother brings back to the den.

The mother cat licks her babies clean. She often moves them to a new den for extra safety.

Useful tails

Like the puma, the domestic cat has a long tail. This helps it to balance as it walks along narrow surfaces, and as it runs.

A mother puma usually has two or three cubs, but there may be as many as six.

3 Lions live in groups

Cat facts

- The male lion is 3 metres long and weighs 200 kilograms.
- The female lion is 2.5 metres long and weighs 130 kilograms.

LIONS are the only kind of cat that live together in a group. All other cats live alone (except for a mother with her babies). A group of lions is called a pride. There are usually between five and ten lions in a pride. They are mostly mothers with their young, and one or two males. Most lions live in Africa, with just a few hundred in India.

In a pride, the chief male lion is the father of all the cubs. His main job is to chase away other lions, so that they cannot steal prey from the pride's area.

The lion is the only big cat where the female and male look different. The male is bigger and has long, shaggy neck fur called a mane.

Padded paws

Lions have thick, leathery pads on the underside of their paws. These help the lion to move quietly and get a good grip on slippery rocks.

Male and female lions roar loudly. This frightens off other lions which aren't in their pride.

4 Jaguars love water

Cat facts

- The jaguar grows up to 2.5 metres long, including its tail.
- It is a heavily built cat and weighs up to 150 kilograms.
- Jaguars live in Central and South America.

Many cats hate water and getting wet. The **JAGUAR** loves it! This big cat is sturdy and strong, with large, powerful muscles. It likes to hunt around rivers, lakes and swamps, and it can swim well. The jaguar catches water creatures such as turtles, caimans (types of crocodiles), crayfish and snakes. It even dives under the surface to chase fish!

After a swim, the jaguar cleans and combs its fur, using its rough tongue and its sharp claws.

American cat!

The jaguar is America's biggest cat. With its spotty coat, it is similar to the leopard of Africa and Asia.

Each 'spot' on the jaguar's coat is like a ring with a dark centre. The patchy pattern helps the jaguar to blend in with leaves and twigs.

The jaguar creeps slowly through water without a splash or a ripple. It surprises prey such as deer and tapirs.

Caracals can leap

Cat facts
• The caracal is about one metre long, including its tail.
• It lives in Africa and the Middle East.

All cats can jump well. But one of the best leapers, for its body size, is the **CARACAL**. It is not a very big cat, yet it can spring forwards more than four metres in one bound. It can even jump three metres in one leap – straight upwards!

The caracal is also called the desert lynx, because it likes dry areas – and because its ears have long tufts of fur like a real lynx.

The caracal eats rats, hares, birds, and baby animals such as antelopes and wild pigs. It also eats lizards and snakes.

The caracal lives in dry places such as rocky hills, grassland, scrub, and around the edges of deserts. Its gold colour makes it difficult to spot among the brown plants and sandy soil.

Champion leap!

The caracal can jump four times its own body length. See how far you can jump – as if you are practising for the long jump!

The caracal crouches down and then springs forwards using its powerful rear legs.

The lynx likes snow

Cat facts

- The lynx is about 1.2 metres long, including its short tail.
- Various kinds of lynx live in the north of Europe, Asia and North America.

The **LYNX** is at home in the snow and ice of the far north. It has very thick fur to keep it warm. Even the tips of its ears have furry tufts. Its paws are large and wide, and they have fur underneath, too. The paws work like snowshoes, to prevent the lynx sinking into soft snow, or sliding on slippery ice.

The lynx has a very short tail, less than 20 centimetres in length. A long tail might get so cold in the freezing winter, that it could suffer from frostbite.

Like many cats, the lynx searches for prey which are old, young, sick, or injured. These are easier to catch than strong, healthy prey!

Snow-paws!

Press your fingers into flour, which is soft and white, like snow. Now put a bag over your hand. See how your 'snow-paw' sinks in less.

The lynx hunts deer, wild sheep and goats, hares and birds. It may bury spare food in the snow and come back to eat it later.

The lynx's paws are wide and furry. They give a good grip on snow, ice, wet rocks and slippery tree branches.

Snow leopards have sharp claws

Cat facts
• The snow leopard lives in the high mountains of central Asia.
• It measures 2 metres long from nose to tail-tip.

The **SNOW LEOPARD**, like other big cats, has five toes on each front foot and four toes on each back foot. Every toe has a sharp claw! The claws grip trees and rocks when climbing, and they slash and slice prey when hunting.

The snow leopard also uses its claws to comb its fur and scratch its skin.

The rare and beautiful snow leopard hunts in mountain forests and crags. It catches wild goats, sheep, birds, monkeys and squirrels.

Smallest cat

The smallest kind of big cat is the clouded leopard of Southeast Asia. It lives almost all of its life in trees.

Like other cats, the snow leopard usually keeps its claws retracted. This means they are pulled back inside its pads, which are like pockets at the ends of its toes. This keeps the claws clean and sharp.

Servals have super-senses!

Cat facts
- The serval is about 1.2 metres long, but it is very slim and weighs only 15 kilograms.
- It lives around lakes and rivers in Africa.

All cats have amazing senses to help them hunt at night. The large eyes of the **SERVAL** see well in the dark. Its long, stiff whiskers help it to feel its way. The serval's big ears pick up sounds and its nose sniffs for food and danger. The serval is unusual for a cat as also hunts by day.

The serval has spots on its body, but stripes on its neck and upper legs.

Cat's eyes!

Cat's eyes have a shiny lining inside them. Some faint light bounces off this lining and makes the eyes glow in the dark.

As the serval pounces, it puts out its claws to hold down the victim. Then it bites with its long, sharp teeth to kill the prey.

The serval has long, slim legs. It peers through the reeds and rushes at the edge of a lake or river, races after its prey — then it pounces!

The serval's favourite meals include swamp rats, water voles and baby ducks.

Leopards have a larder

Cat facts

• The leopard lives in many regions across Africa and southern Asia.

• It is about 2.5 metres in total length.

Sometimes a cat like the **LEOPARD** catches prey which is too big to eat in one meal. So the leopard stores the leftovers up in a tree. Here they are kept safe from hungry hyaenas and jackals too!

Leopards live in lots of places, from dry grassland and scrub to mountains, forests and swamps. They even live around villages.

The leopard may wait on a branch, and then pounce silently on a victim below.

Every leopard has a different pattern of spots – just like every person has different fingerprints.

Black leopard!

The black panther is not a different kind of big cat. It's a leopard with very dark fur.

The leopard's favourite tree has scratch marks in the bark. They warn other leopards to keep away.

The leopard is strong enough to drag a whole gazelle up into a tree.

A leopard can catch large animals such as antelopes, which are three times its own size. When food is scarce, it will eat rats, mice, birds' eggs, and even insects such as beetles!

Cat facts
• The cheetah measures about 2 metres from nose to tail.

No animal can run as fast as the **CHEETAH**. This big cat races along at 100 kilometres per hour – almost as fast as a car on a motorway. The cheetah can only keep up this speed for half a minute. Then it must stop to cool down and get its breath back.

Cheetahs hunt small gazelles, antelopes, hares and other fast-running animals.

• It lives in Africa and western Asia.

The cheetah tries to trip or knock over its victim, then pounces on it.

Cheetahs and many other kinds of big cat have become rare. Once, cats were killed for their fur, to make coats and hats. Today, all cats need our help to survive.

The cheetah likes dry, open places such as grassland and scrub. It cannot run very fast in a thick wood!

Claws out!

The cheetah is the only cat which cannot pull its claws into its toes. The claws are big and blunt, like a dog's.

The cheetah has a small head, a slim and bendy body, and very long legs.

Index